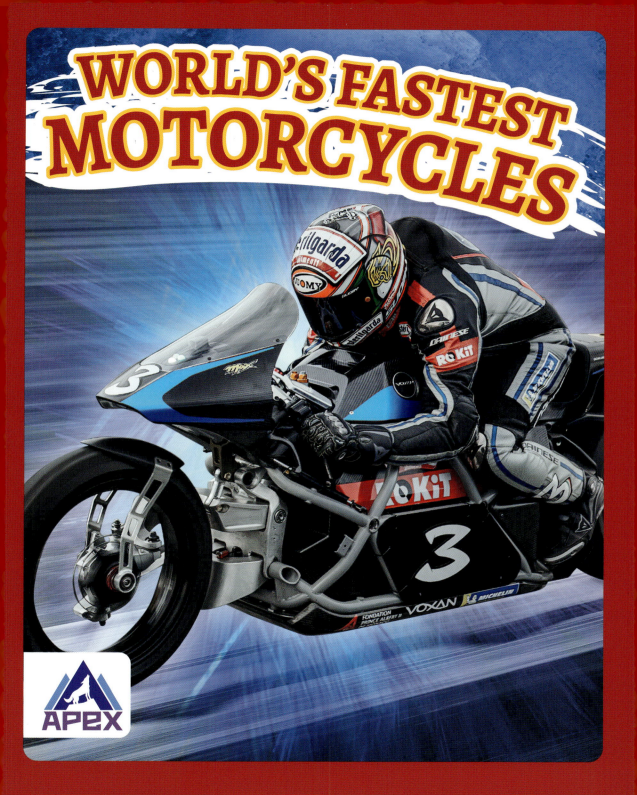

WORLD'S FASTEST MOTORCYCLES

BY HUBERT WALKER

WWW.APEXEDITIONS.COM

Copyright © 2022 by Apex Editions, Mendota Heights, MN 55120. All rights reserved. No part of this book may be reproduced or utilized in any form or by any means without written permission from the publisher.

Apex is distributed by North Star Editions:
sales@northstareditions.com | 888-417-0195

Produced for Apex by Red Line Editorial.

Photographs ©: Voxan/Cover Images/AP Images, cover, 1, 26–27; Shutterstock Images, 4–5, 6–7, 8–9, 13, 14–15, 15, 16–17, 18–19, 20, 20–21, 22–23, 24–25, 25, 29; iStockphoto, 10–11; George Grantham Bain Collection/Library of Congress, 12

Library of Congress Control Number: 2021918464

ISBN
978-1-63738-171-7 (hardcover)
978-1-63738-207-3 (paperback)
978-1-63738-275-2 (ebook pdf)
978-1-63738-243-1 (hosted ebook)

Printed in the United States of America
Mankato, MN
012022

NOTE TO PARENTS AND EDUCATORS

Apex books are designed to build literacy skills in striving readers. Exciting, high-interest content attracts and holds readers' attention. The text is carefully leveled to allow students to achieve success quickly. Additional features, such as bolded glossary words for difficult terms, help build comprehension.

TABLE OF CONTENTS

CHAPTER 1
BUILT FOR SPEED   5

CHAPTER 2
MOTORCYCLE HISTORY   11

CHAPTER 3
MORE POWER   17

CHAPTER 4
REACHING TOP SPEED   23

Comprehension Questions • 28

Glossary • 30

To Learn More • 31

About the Author • 31

Index • 32

CHAPTER 1

BUILT FOR SPEED

A rider climbs onto his Kawasaki Ninja H2R. Then he twists the **throttle** and takes off. The **sleek** motorcycle roars with power.

The 2021 version of the Kawasaki Ninja H2R cost $55,500.

The rider shifts into high **gear**. The Ninja streaks across a long bridge. For safety, the bridge is closed to traffic.

The Ninja H2R set its speed record on the Osman Gazi Bridge in Turkey.

The world's fastest motorcycles are known as superbikes.

Soon, the bike reaches top speed. It hits 248 miles per hour (400 km/h). The Ninja H2R is one of the fastest motorcycles in the world.

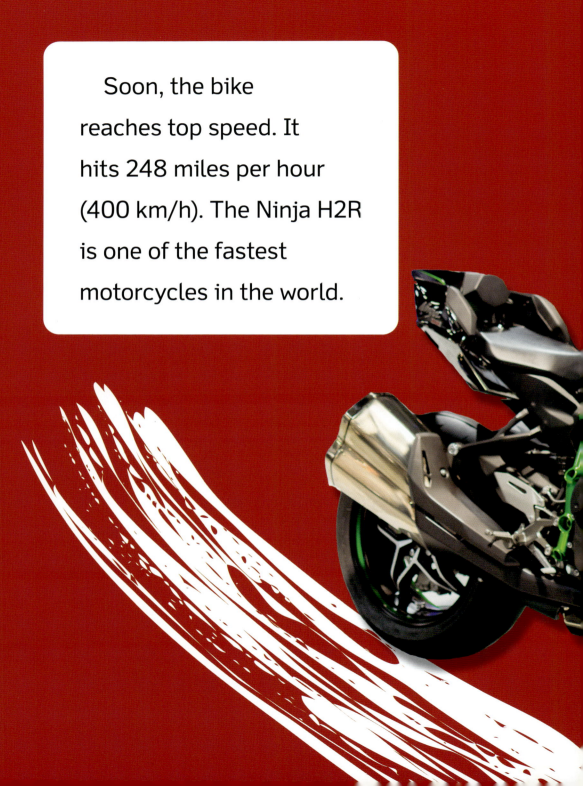

STREET LEGAL

The Ninja H2R is a racing bike. Kawasaki also makes a version that is **legal** to drive on the street. It is called the Ninja H2.

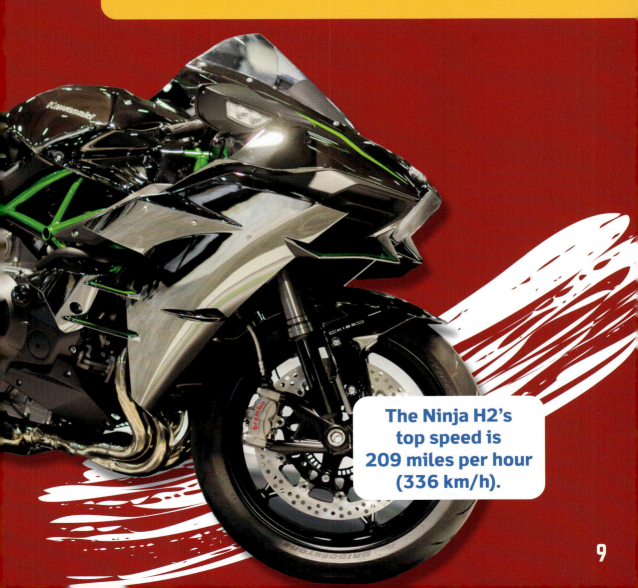

The Ninja H2's top speed is 209 miles per hour (336 km/h).

CHAPTER 2
MOTORCYCLE HISTORY

The world's first motorcycle came out in 1894. It was made in Germany. This bike had a top speed of 28 miles per hour (45 km/h).

The first motorcycle was called the Hildebrand & Wolfmüller.

Motorcycles improved quickly. By 1925, the fastest bike could top 100 miles per hour (161 km/h).

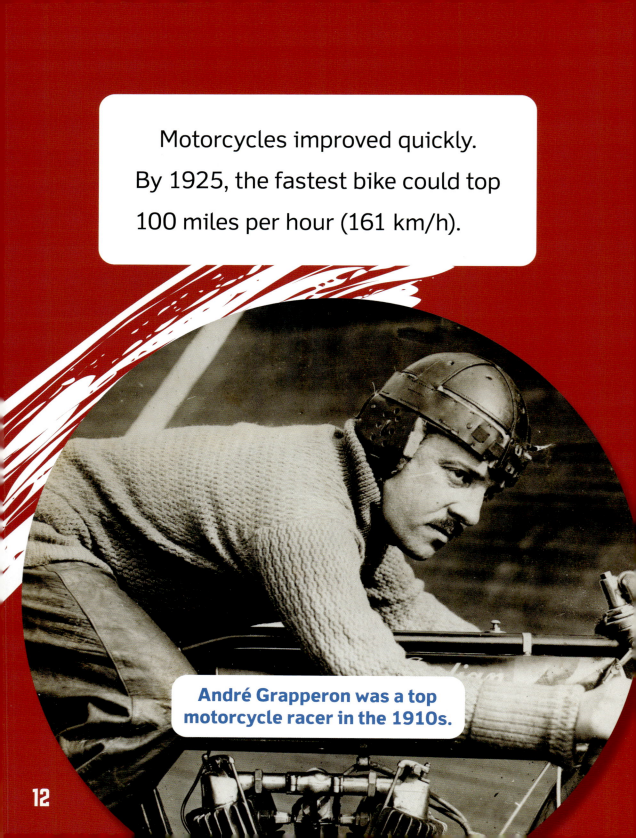

André Grapperon was a top motorcycle racer in the 1910s.

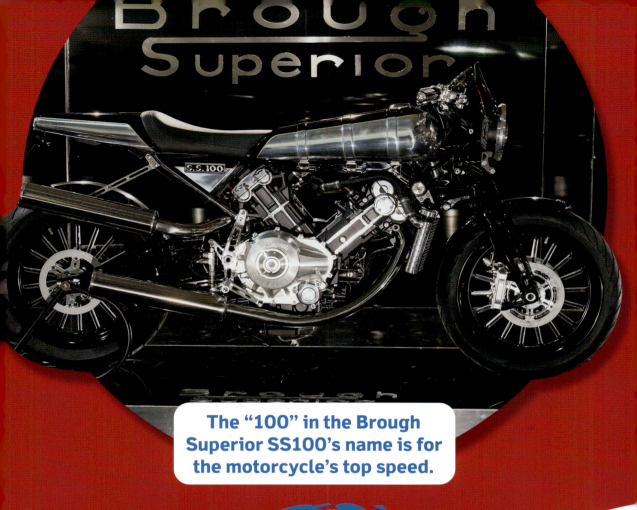

The "100" in the Brough Superior SS100's name is for the motorcycle's top speed.

The Brough Superior SS100 was the first motorcycle to reach 100 miles per hour (161 km/h).

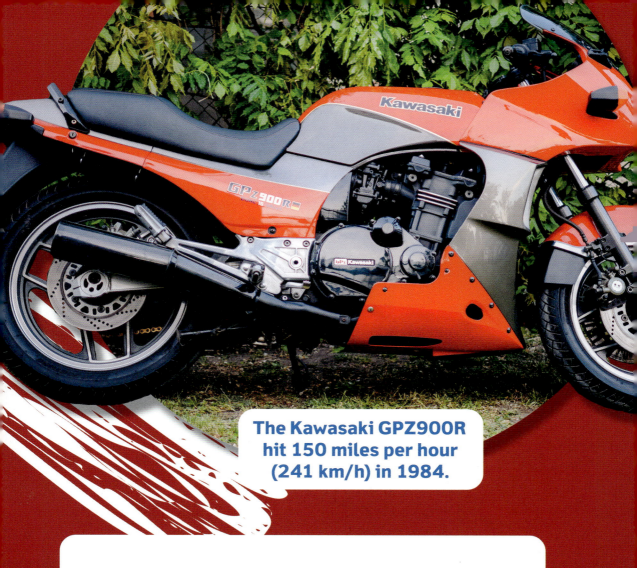

The Kawasaki GPZ900R hit 150 miles per hour (241 km/h) in 1984.

Motorcycle **designers** didn't stop there. They continued to push the limits. By the 1980s, superbikes could reach 150 miles per hour (241 km/h).

JAPANESE DESIGN

In the late 1900s, the fastest motorcycles often came from Japan. Kawasaki, Honda, and Suzuki were three top companies. They all competed to make the fastest bike.

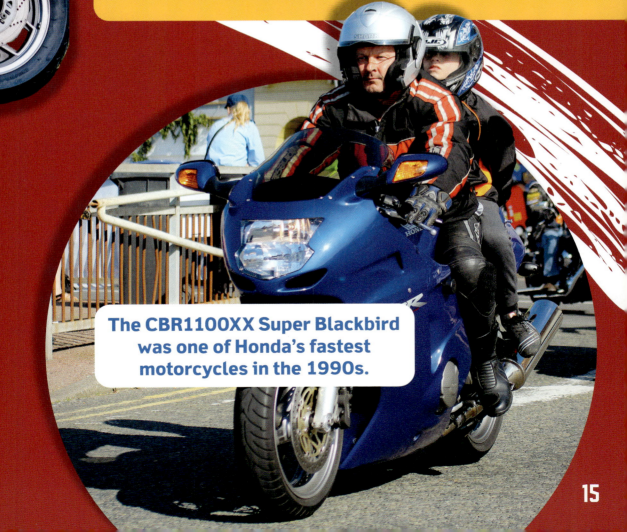

The CBR1100XX Super Blackbird was one of Honda's fastest motorcycles in the 1990s.

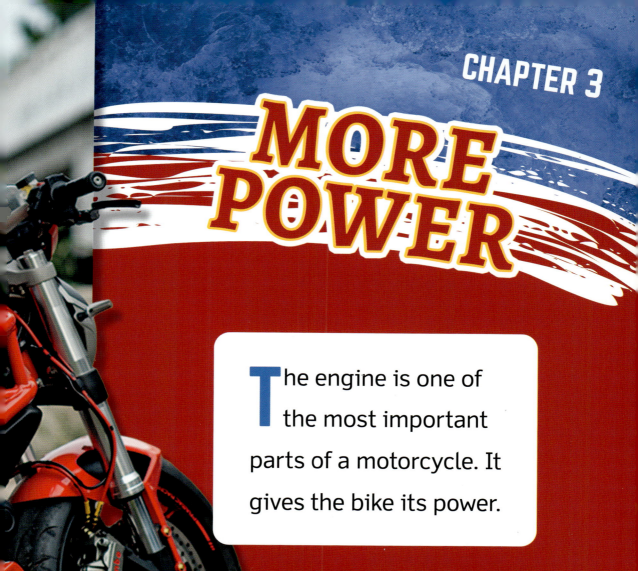

CHAPTER 3
MORE POWER

The engine is one of the most important parts of a motorcycle. It gives the bike its power.

Ducati's motorcycles often have very powerful engines.

Many of the best motorcycles have **superchargers**. These parts help bikes **accelerate** faster.

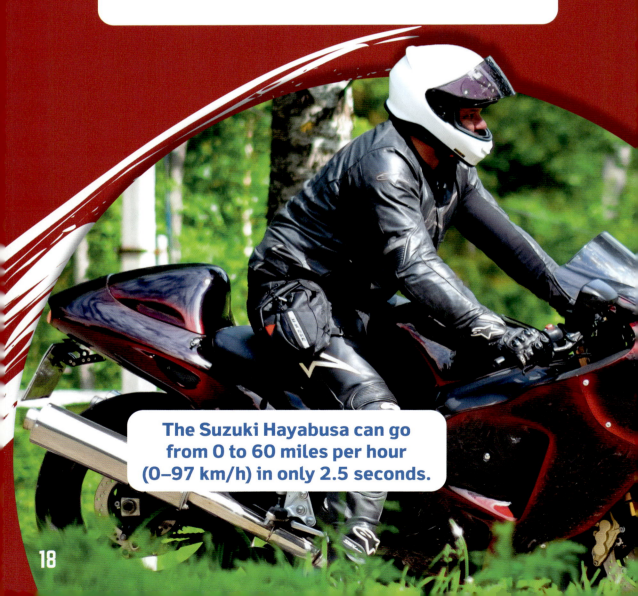

The Suzuki Hayabusa can go from 0 to 60 miles per hour (0–97 km/h) in only 2.5 seconds.

SPEED LIMITERS

In the 2000s, several companies made an agreement. They put speed limiters on their motorcycles. These parts kept bikes from going faster than 186 miles per hour (300 km/h).

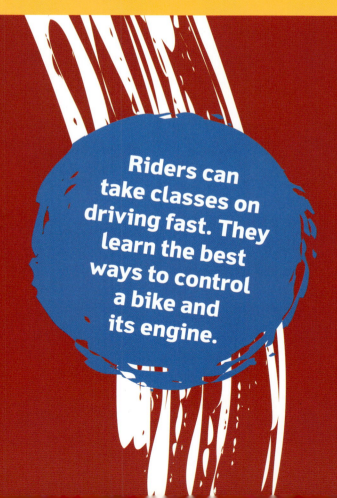

Riders can take classes on driving fast. They learn the best ways to control a bike and its engine.

Many bikes have mudguards made from carbon fiber. These parts block dirt and rocks kicked up by the bike's tires.

Fast motorcycles must also be light. Some companies make bikes out of carbon fiber. This material is very strong. But it is also very light.

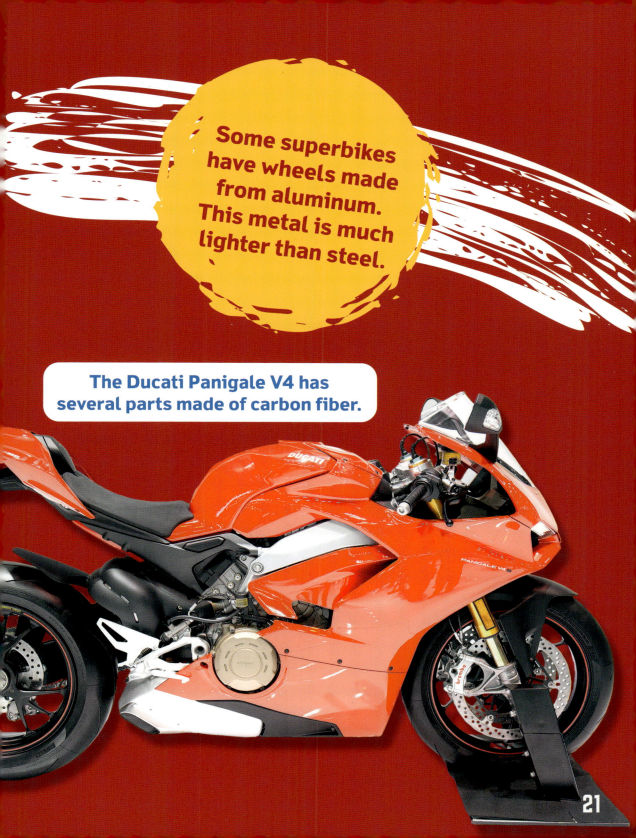

Some superbikes have wheels made from aluminum. This metal is much lighter than steel.

The Ducati Panigale V4 has several parts made of carbon fiber.

CHAPTER 4
REACHING TOP SPEED

The shape of a motorcycle also matters. A bike must be able to cut through the air. That's why superbikes have sleek designs.

To go even faster, riders often hunch close to their bikes.

23

Gearing is important, too. Gearing is what makes power go from the engine to the rear wheel. Most motorcycles have six gears.

The part that holds a bike's gears together is called the gearbox.

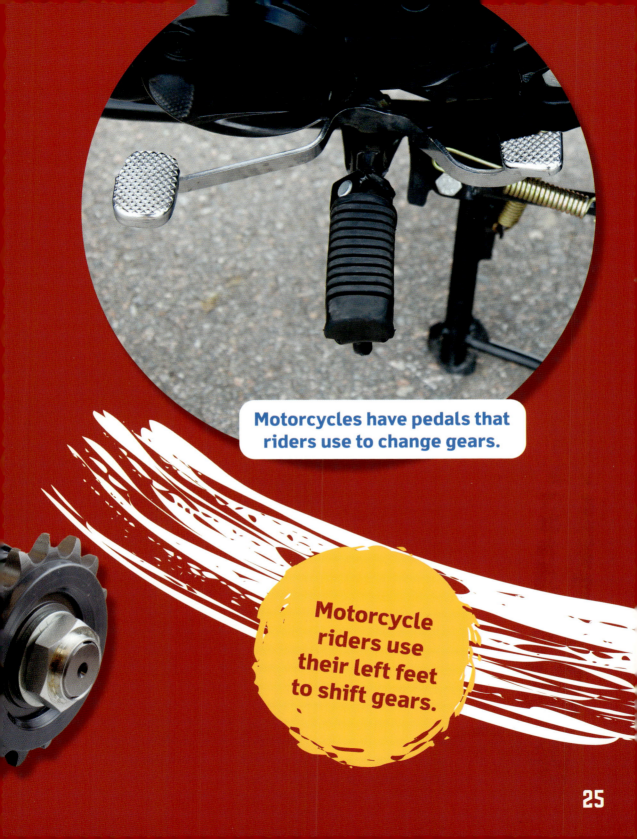

Motorcycles have pedals that riders use to change gears.

Motorcycle riders use their left feet to shift gears.

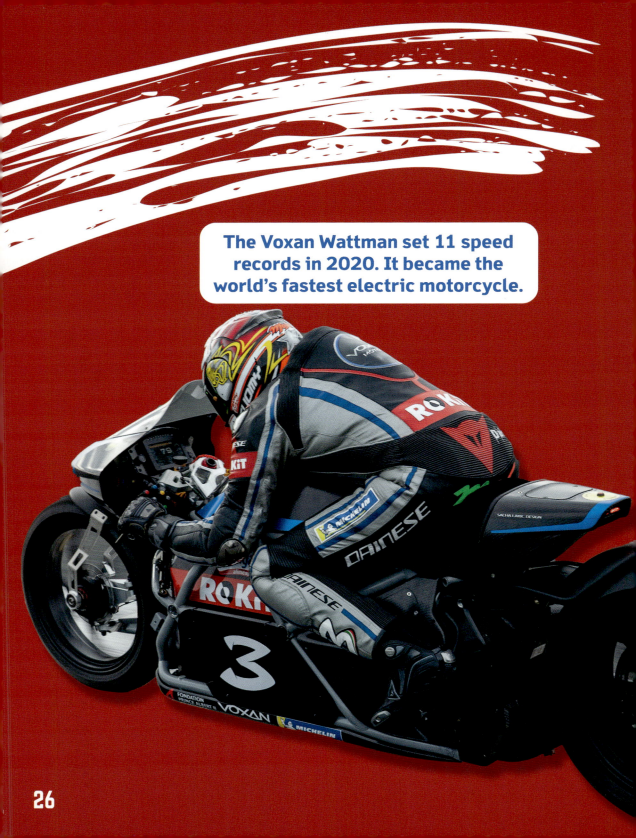

The Voxan Wattman set 11 speed records in 2020. It became the world's fastest electric motorcycle.

Some superbikes do not use **gasoline**. For example, the Voxan Wattman is powered by electricity. It can reach speeds of 231 miles per hour (372 km/h).

NO LIMITS

In the 2010s, some companies stopped using speed limiters. As a result, superbikes could go faster than ever. One example is the Lightning LS-218. This electric bike can go 218 miles per hour (351 km/h).

COMPREHENSION QUESTIONS

Write your answers on a separate piece of paper.

1. Write a few sentences explaining the main ideas of Chapter 3.

2. Do you think superbikes should have speed limiters? Why or why not?

3. When did the world's first motorcycle come out?

    A. 1894
    B. 1925
    C. 1980

4. What would happen if a motorcycle did not have a supercharger?

    A. The bike would not be able to cut through the air.
    B. The bike would not gain speed as quickly.
    C. The bike would be too heavy to ride.

5. What does **streaks** mean in this book?

*The rider shifts into high gear. The Ninja **streaks** across a long bridge.*

    A. falls apart
    B. travels slowly
    C. moves at a fast speed

6. What does **competed** mean in this book?

*Kawasaki, Honda, and Suzuki were three top companies. They all **competed** to make the fastest bike.*

    A. tried to be the best
    B. stopped making motorcycles
    C. cheated to win

Answer key on page 32.

GLOSSARY

accelerate
To speed up.

designers
People who come up with new ideas for products.

gasoline
A fuel made from oil. Gasoline can be burned for energy.

gear
A setting on a vehicle that controls how fast it can go. A gear controls how power moves from the vehicle's engine to its wheels.

legal
Allowed by law.

sleek
Having a shape that cuts through the air.

superchargers
Parts that push more air into engines, helping the engines produce more power.

throttle
A motorcycle part that lets the rider control how much fuel enters the engine.

TO LEARN MORE

BOOKS

Hamilton, S. L. *The World's Fastest Motorcycles*. Minneapolis: Abdo Publishing, 2021.

Klepeis, Alicia Z. *Superfast Motorcycles*. Minneapolis: Jump!, 2022.

Slingerland, Janet. *Superfast Motorcycle Racing*. Minneapolis: Lerner Publications, 2020.

ONLINE RESOURCES

Visit **www.apexeditions.com** to find links and resources related to this title.

ABOUT THE AUTHOR

Hubert Walker enjoys running, hunting, and going to the dog park with his best pal. He grew up in Georgia but moved to Minnesota in 2018. Overall, he loves his new home, but he's not a fan of the cold winters.

INDEX

B
Brough Superior SS100, 13

C
carbon fiber, 20

D
designers, 14

E
engines, 17, 19, 24

G
gears, 6, 24–25
Germany, 11

H
Honda, 15

J
Japan, 15

K
Kawasaki, 5, 9, 15
Kawasaki Ninja H2, 9
Kawasaki Ninja H2R, 5–6, 8–9

L
Lightning LS-218, 27

S
speed limiters, 19, 27
superbikes, 7, 14, 21, 23, 27
superchargers, 18
Suzuki, 15

T
throttle, 5

V
Voxan Wattman, 27

Answer Key:
1. Answers will vary; **2.** Answers will vary; **3.** A; **4.** B; **5.** C; **6.** A